TANZANIA

in pictures

By JOEL REUBEN
and HOWARD CARSTENS

VISUAL
GEOGRAPHY
SERIES

 STERLING
PUBLISHING CO., INC.   NEW YORK

 Oak Tree Press Co., Ltd.
London & Sydney

VISUAL GEOGRAPHY SERIES

Afghanistan
Alaska
Argentina
Australia
Austria
Belgium and Luxembourg
Berlin—East and West
Brazil
Bulgaria
Canada
The Caribbean (English-
  Speaking Islands)
Ceylon
Chile
Colombia
Czechoslovakia
Denmark

Ecuador
England
Ethiopia
Fiji
Finland
France
French Canada
Ghana
Greece
Guatemala
Hawaii
Holland
Honduras
Hong Kong
Hungary
Iceland
India

Indonesia
Iran
Iraq
Ireland
Islands of the
  Mediterranean
Israel
Italy
Jamaica
Japan
Kenya
Korea
Kuwait
Lebanon
Liberia
Malaysia and Singapore

Mexico
Morocco
Nepal
New Zealand
Norway
Pakistan
Panama and the Canal
  Zone
Peru
The Philippines
Poland
Portugal
Puerto Rico
Rumania
Russia
Scotland

South Africa
Spain
Surinam
Sweden
Switzerland
Tahiti and the
  French Islands of
  the Pacific
Taiwan
Tanzania
Thailand
Turkey
Venezuela
Wales
West Germany
Yugoslavia

PICTURE CREDITS

The authors and publisher wish to thank the following organizations for the photographs used in this book: B.O.A.C.; Tanganyika Coffee Board; Tanganyika Information Services; Tanzania Information Services; Tanzania National Tourist Board; Tanzania Tourist Corporation; Tanzania Tourist Office.

Copyright © 1972 by Sterling Publishing Co., Inc.
419 Park Avenue South, New York, N.Y. 10016
British edition published by Oak Tree Press Co., Ltd., Nassau, Bahamas
Distributed in Australia by Oak Tree Press Co., Ltd.,
P.O. Box 34, Brickfield Hill, Sydney 2000, N.S.W.
Distributed in the United Kingdom and elsewhere in the British Commonwealth
by Ward Lock Ltd., 116 Baker Street, London W 1
Manufactured in the United States of America
Library of Congress Catalog Card No.: 78-180453
ISBN 0-8069-1154-9   UK 7061 2361-1
1155-7

In areas suffering from food shortages, able-bodied men are given jobs such as road-making. In return, they receive free rations of food. They are only required to work for a few hours to qualify for this relief aid. In the background can be seen a baobab tree.

CONTENTS   1738170

INTRODUCTION 5
1. THE LAND 7
    TOPOGRAPHY . . . RIVERS AND LAKES . . . CLIMATE . . . NATURAL RESOURCES
    . . . CITIES AND TOWNS . . . FLORA . . . FAUNA . . . Serengeti National
    Park . . . Ngorongoro Crater . . . Other Animals . . . OLDUVAI GORGE
2. HISTORY 20
    THE PORTUGUESE . . . THE 18TH AND 19TH CENTURIES . . . Missionary
    Activity . . . EXPLORING THE INTERIOR . . . GERMAN INVOLVEMENT . . .
    WORLD WAR I AND ITS AFTERMATH . . . TANGANYIKA AS A U.N. TRUSTEE-
    SHIP . . . JULIUS NYERERE AND TANU . . . Events Leading to Independence
    . . . SELF-GOVERNMENT AND INDEPENDENCE . . . UNION BETWEEN TAN-
    GANYIKA AND ZANZIBAR
3. GOVERNMENT AND SOCIAL SERVICES 33
    PHILOSOPHY OF THE GOVERNMENT . . . ONE-PARTY SYSTEM . . . NATIONALI-
    ZATION POLICIES . . . NEUTRALITY, NATIONALISM AND PAN-AFRICANISM . . .
    EAST AFRICAN CO-OPERATION . . . HEALTH AND EDUCATION
4. THE PEOPLE 44
    AFRICANS . . . Central Highland Peoples . . . Family Customs . . . Village
    Life . . . City Life . . . EASTERN TANZANIA PEOPLE . . . Family Customs and
    Village Life . . . COASTAL PEOPLES . . . Village Life . . . City Life . . . THE
    PEOPLE OF THE NORTH . . . The Chaggas . . . The Masai . . . LANGUAGES . . .
    MODERN TANZANIA
5. THE ECONOMY 54
    AGRICULTURE . . . MINERAL WEALTH . . . EXPORTS . . . FORESTS . . . LIVE-
    STOCK . . . ZANZIBAR'S ECONOMY . . . TOURISM IN TANZANIA

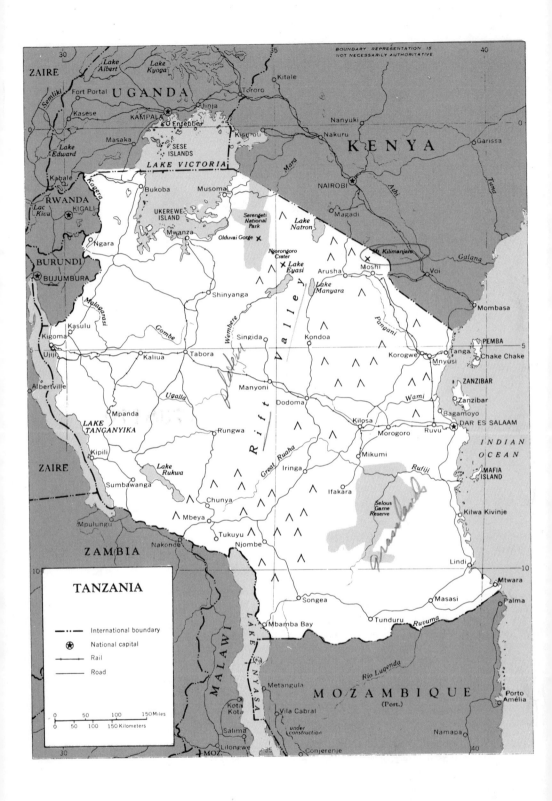

TANZANIA

-·-·-·- International boundary
⊛ National capital
+—+—+ Rail
——— Road

0   50   100   150 Miles
0 50 100 150 Kilometers

A tribesman (white spot in foreground) of the Chunya region strolls on the edge of the escarpment overlooking the western Rift Valley. The escarpment is over a mile above sea level and the valley floor is about 3,000 feet in elevation.

INTRODUCTION

THE NEW NATION of Tanzania (pronounced Tan-zan-EE-a rather than the often heard but incorrect Tan-ZANE-e-ya) forms with the countries of Kenya and Uganda the region called East Africa. Tanzania shares a somewhat similar geography and history with the other nations of East Africa and yet when one looks at Tanzania more closely it becomes obvious that this nation differs markedly from the others. Tanzania is by far the largest in area and the least densely populated. The people and the economy of Tanzania are the poorest and least developed in East Africa. Whereas Kenya and Uganda are dominated by large tribes such as the Kikuyu, Luo and the Buganda (numbering in the millions), Tanzania, with 13,000,000 people, has over 100 tribes with only nineteen numbering over 100,000.

Language is still another area in which the people and government of Tanzania have taken a different course from Uganda and Kenya.

Swahili, a language whose roots are Arabic and Bantu, has become the *lingua franca* of Tanzania. Unlike Kenya and Uganda, where vernacular (tribal) languages are encouraged and English is the language of the educated élite, Tanzania has taken the lead in preserving Swahili, so that it is spoken by some 30,000,000 Africans as far north as Ethiopia and as far south along the east coast of the continent as Mozambique.

Although Tanzania has historical similarities with Kenya and Uganda, its history in the last century is linked to Germany rather than England, which colonized the other nations of East Africa. It is interesting to note that Tanzania was not coveted by the major colonial powers as was Uganda. Germany only became interested in the area (called Tanganyika at that time) because the other nations of Europe were so far ahead in the race for colonies. In fact, after Germany was defeated in World War I and its colonies in Africa were taken away, no one

5

wanted the responsibility of taking care of the land that is today Tanzania. Both England and Belgium refused the offer. Finally, while Kenya and Uganda to the north were being settled and developed by England, Tanganyika was placed under the care of the League of Nations and later the United Nations.

Just as Tanzania is unique in terms of geography, history and language, it appears to be quite different politically in the East African context. When independence came to Tanzania in 1961, the people elected a schoolteacher to be their first president. In Kenya and Uganda, politicians and freedom-fighters were elected to run these nations. The uniqueness of Tanzania continues today in terms of its foreign policy. While Kenya and Uganda attempt to be neutral in foreign affairs, they remain loyal to the Western bloc countries which are their chief suppliers of aid and technology. Tanzania, on the other hand, straddles the fence between East and West, accepting aid and technical assistance from Communist China, the Soviet Union, the United States and Great Britain. In addition, Tanzania serves as a haven for African exiles and freedom units from all over the continent.

Many authorities on Africa believe that Tanzania is one of the most exciting countries on the continent. Its determination to build a new and better nation is very great. Led by its president, Julius Nyerere, affectionately called "Mwalimu" or "Teacher" by his people, Tanzania is attempting to live up to its motto "UHURU NA UMOJA" which translates to "Freedom and Oneness."

An island a few hundred yards from the Tanzanian port of Mwanza on Lake Victoria is now a permanent sanctuary for wildlife. Giraffes, elephants, zebras and deer wander freely among the rocks and by the shore. Other animals—rhinoceroses, buffaloes and wild dogs—live in enclosures. The island is called Saanane, which is Swahili for "Eight o'clock," and was the name of an African farmer who once made it his home.

The king of beasts surveys his domain.

I. THE LAND

THE UNITED REPUBLIC of Tanzania is located on the east coast of Africa, just below the equator. It is a large country—larger than France and Italy together, or Texas and Oklahoma combined.

The mainland portion, formerly called Tanganyika, is nearly 362,000 square miles in area. The island portions are Zanzibar, and the smaller islands of Pemba, Mafia, Latham, and several others along the coast. Zanzibar and the other islands cover about 1,200 square miles. The surrounding countries are Kenya on the north; Uganda, Rwanda, Burundi, and Zaire (formerly the Democratic Republic of the Congo) on the west; and Zambia, Malawi, and Mozambique on the south. To the east is the Indian Ocean.

Tanzania is a country of great contrasts, containing the continent's tallest mountain (Kilimanjaro), the deepest lake (Tanganyika), and the world's largest wild game reserve (Selous). Of the 13,000,000 people in Tanzania only 5 per cent live in cities or large towns. The population is most dense around the edges of the country and sparse in the central region. The economy is almost entirely agricultural, and most people are farmers. Crops are raised from sea level up to 8,000-foot elevations.

A clear view of Kibo peak on Mt. Kilimanjaro is uncommon—usually the mountain is hidden by a ring of clouds. The scrub and grass in the foreground give way to heavy forests higher up the slopes of the mountain.

TOPOGRAPHY

Mainland Tanzania has a long and beautiful coastline on the Indian Ocean, protected by many coral reefs. The coastal plain is narrow—only 20 miles wide and about 500 miles long. The coastal plain rises sharply to a plateau averaging about 3,500 feet above sea level.

In the central and southern regions the land rises more gradually to high grasslands and to the mountain ranges called the Southern Highlands. The whole country is parted from

The famous Bismarck Rocks, named after the German statesman who was instrumental in making Tanganyika a German colony, are located on the shore of Lake Victoria. Steamer service between the East African nations includes stops at the Tanzanian towns of Musoma, Mwanza and Bukoba.

One of the most numerous and lovely birds in Tanzania is the flamingo. Seen here is a large flock inhabiting a small lake in the middle of Ngorongoro Crater. Other birds in Tanzania include egrets, ibises and storks in lake areas, and kingfishers, larks and plovers in the woodlands.

north to south by the Great Rift Valley which is a huge trough in the earth's surface running over 3,000 miles from Syria south to Mozambique. The walls of the rift are several thousand feet above the floor at many points.

In the north, elevations are highest—and there in the Moshi district close to Kenya, is Mt. Kilimanjaro, the roof of all Africa. It is formed by three volcanic mountains: Shira, the oldest, is 13,140 feet, Mwanzi is 16,900 feet, and Kibo, the youngest, is 19,340 feet tall. Many people come to see Kilimanjaro with its perpetual ring of clouds and permanent ice cap so near the equator. The surrounding countryside is a fertile plateau with a pleasant climate.

RIVERS AND LAKES

Small lakes on the central Rift floor have been evaporating over the centuries, and vast deposits of sodium carbonate have been left. Flamingos have found some of the lakes to be a breeding ground, and hundreds of thousands of these brilliant pink birds can be seen on the lake shores.

A western branch of the Great Rift Valley is filled with deep, clear lakes swarming with fish. These lakes form much of Tanzania's western border. Lake Tanganyika lies on the border with Zaire, and Lake Nyasa lies on the border with Malawi. Lake Tanganyika's floor is 4,730 feet under water and 2,300 feet below sea level. By volume, this is the third largest fresh-water lake in the world.

Between the two branches of the Rift is Lake Victoria, famed as the headwaters of the River Nile and the second largest fresh-water lake by area in the world, after Lake Superior in North America. In Lake Victoria, the borders of Kenya, Uganda, and Tanzania meet, at an elevation of 3,700 feet. Most of the rivers are unimportant—yet the sources of Africa's three greatest rivers, the Nile, the Congo and the Zambezi are all in Tanzania!

Some rivers in Tanzania's dry areas flow only during the rainy season. Along the coast, many small streams flow into the Indian Ocean. The

is rapid. The temperatures are pleasant inland because of the high altitude, but along the coast the temperatures reach the mid-90's. Because of the closeness to the equator there is no noticeable difference between "winter" and "summer."

NATURAL RESOURCES

Over half of the country's wealth comes from agricultural products, so that the soil has to be considered Tanzania's most important natural resource. Most of the land is *latosolic*, or lacking in rich humus and subject to alternating wet and dry cycles. Rain sinks rapidly into the soil, a fact which makes water supply a problem. Where there is steady rainfall, thick forests grow.

Tanzania has been blessed by nature with more mineral wealth than other East African countries. Diamonds are the country's most important mineral. Gold is the second most

largest river system in East Africa is the great Ruaha-Rufiji, which drains from the Rift Valley into the Indian Ocean, and is navigable from the coast for about 60 miles.

CLIMATE

In general, Tanzanians relate their weather to the rainy season—"Will it come on time, and will there be enough?" The monsoon winds blow from the northeast from October to February, and from the southwest the remainder of the year. December is the rainiest month in most of the country, but in the northeast and along the coast a second rainy season begins in March or April.

Rainfall in Tanzania ranges from over 40 inches per year along the coast and around Lake Victoria, to 10 inches in the central plateau. This may be compared with London's 41 inches and San Francisco's 20 inches. The sun's rays penetrate the atmosphere more easily at the tropical latitudes, and evaporation

These boys of the Tanga region have caught a spiny lobster or sea crayfish, near the mouth of the Pangani River.

The Amboni Caves, located 9 miles from Tanga, are vast underground limestone formations. Nearby there are numerous sulphur springs.

In a narrow street in Zanzibar town, a fruit stall attracts customers. These same streets were the scene of a violent revolution in 1964, before Zanzibar was united with Tanganyika.

important, and there are also working mines for other gem stones, salt, mica, and tin.

CITIES AND TOWNS

The largest city and capital of Tanzania is Dar es Salaam, whose name is Arabic for "haven of peace." Its population in 1970 was estimated at more than 300,000. Dar, as it is called for short, is a deep-water port connected by rail with Tanga, Arusha, and Kenya to the north, with Mwanza on Lake Victoria, to the northwest, and with Kigoma on Lake Tanganyika, to the west. Dar is a city with its own character, and considerably different from the other East African capitals, Nairobi and Kampala. The waterfront and the streets are lined with stately palms, and there are excellent hotels for visitors.

Tanga is a city of 39,000 people located at the terminus of the rail line, where sisal is transferred to the ships in port. It is also a holiday and fishing hub for Tanzanians in the northeast. Mwanza is a city of 20,000 people on the south of Lake Victoria. The rail line connects here with the Lake Victoria steamer to Kisumu in Kenya and Entebbe in Uganda. Zanzibar town is populated by 58,000 persons and is Arab in character. Its narrow streets pass by many beautiful Arab carved doorways which the government has ruled will be preserved.

Smaller towns between 10,000 and 20,000 people are Moshi in the north and Mtwara on the south coast. Morogoro, Dodoma, and Iringa are the principal towns in the central highlands.

Arusha has a special rôle as a city of Tanzania and East Africa. It is located at the geographical midpoint of East Africa and was named the headquarters of the East African Common Services Organization serving Kenya, Uganda, and Tanzania. With a population of 12,000, it is headquarters for the safari business in northern Tanzania, a railhead for Dar, and a fuel stop on the road to Nairobi in Kenya. It was here that President Nyerere chose to deliver his famous declaration of February, 1967.

Dar es Salaam, the capital and most important city of Tanzania, is more African in quality than the European-style capitals of Kenya and Uganda. The city has grown tremendously in recent years and today is a thriving port.

Kigoma, a town on the shores of Lake Tanganyika only a few miles from the site of the historic meeting of Stanley and Livingstone, is one of the best fishing grounds in Tanzania.

13

Mt. Meru, located near the northern town of Arusha, is an extinct volcano rising over 18,000 feet. Nearby is the newest of Tanzania's 12 great game parks, Arusha National Park. This park includes the mountain, a giant crater stocked with game, and the picturesque Momella Lakes. The blossom in the foreground is a moonflower.

FLORA

The contrasts of Tanzania are vividly illustrated in its varied plant life. On the coast, coconut palms and cashew trees are plentiful, while inland the flora turns to "miombo" trees, grasses, bottle-shaped baobabs (or "monkey bread" trees), thorn trees, and sometimes luxuriant woodlands. Often the vegetation covers the hills to the top, and finding one's way can be a problem. Sometimes the hiker finds a tall rock formation jutting into the sky high enough for him to climb and get his bearings again.

On the slopes of the mountains are thick rain forests, rising from about 5,000 feet, and including the South African yellowwood and various species of cedar. Around the highest peaks are bamboo, lichen, the flowered spikes of lobelias, and groundsels that resemble giant cabbages.

There is a stretch of gradually rising land that occurs 20 miles or more inland, which the African calls the *Nyika*—a wilderness of bushland, dry river beds, rocky hills, and the giant baobab tree. Here the delicate balance of nature is challenged by big game and the dry seasons. Elephants uproot the trees in order to get at the top choice leaves which they could not reach otherwise. Grasses take the place of the uprooted trees, and then during the dry season fire chars it all, and nature must start anew.

14

Many giraffes live in the national park surrounding Manyara Lake in the central Rift Valley. These animals occasionally reach 16 feet in height and have highly developed circulatory systems which enable them to pump blood up their necks in stages in order not to overtax the heart.

FAUNA

Most visitors to Tanzania return to their homelands impressed by the sight of vast lands yet unspoiled by an industrial society. These are lands which, if they can survive the crush of population, will reveal new insights to students who seek to understand man's place in nature.

Perhaps the most thrilling sight to a visitor is found in Tanzania's wildlife, for the country is the largest refuge of wildlife left in the world. The Tanzanian government has worked diligently to reconcile the demands of man for land to farm and the needs of wildlife for plenty of space, and has established 12 national parks

The shy vervet, found in southern and eastern Africa, is quite active when roused. These monkeys have brownish-green fur and black hands, feet and faces. Besides vervets, Tanzania also has a large number of colobus monkeys, whose fur is quite valuable.

A pair of male lions spend the sunny midday in the shade of a thorn tree. A pride (family) of lions will search for food every two or three days. The females make the kill, stand by while the males eat, and bring in the cubs to finish the meal.

The wildebeest, or gnu, inhabits the northern plains of Tanzania, moving from place to place looking for green grass and surface water supplies. In order to escape from enemies, the wildebeest can get up speed very quickly.

Zebras graze in the Ngorongoro Crater National Park. The zigzag trail in the background is used by visitors who descend from the lodge on the crater's rim for a day of viewing game. Land Rovers are used, as the grade is steep and the surface often muddy.

A leopard rests and watches for game from a perch in a euphorbia tree (resembling a giant cactus). The leopard weighs about 125 pounds and climbs trees with ease, often hiding its kill high among the branches.

The vast, flat floor of Ngorongoro Crater is a refuge for game of all types.

and game preserves where many varied types of animals live naturally. Here rhinoceroses, elephants, lions, cheetahs, leopards, giraffes, buffaloes, zebras and ostriches abound, along

While the elders of the pride sleep, lion cubs of different ages play and nurse.

After the lion and the leopard eat their fill, the vultures move in to finish off the carcass.

with a bewildering variety of antelopes. In the streams and lakes are the lazy hippopotamus and the fierce crocodile.

SERENGETI NATIONAL PARK

This 5,000-square-mile expanse of northern Tanzania, which varies between treeless savannah and thick forest, houses 1,500,000 large mammals. At times a quarter of a million gazelles and zebras can be seen moving in long lines towards a new supply of ground water near the M'balagetti and Mara Rivers. The game here represent a complete spectrum from grass-eaters to meat-eaters. The park management estimates that over 35 species of plains game and 350 species of birds are to be found in the Serengeti.

NGORONGORO CRATER

This extinct crater, also in northern Tanzania, has walls about 7,000 feet high and a floor 2,000 feet below the surface. It measures 12 miles across. Ngorongoro Crater is the home of the largest permanent population of game in all Africa. Observers wind their way down the paths to the floor to study the habits of handsome brown-maned lions, crafty lightning-swift cheetahs, hyenas, and the great herds of plains game on which they prey.

OTHER ANIMALS

A rarity in Tanzania, the chimpanzee is found only in the highlands near Lake Tanganyika. Many small mammals are native—flying foxes, civets, servals (a kind of wildcat), monkeys and rodents in profusion, and the hyrax—a small creature that climbs trees, but is actually an ungulate, or hoofed, animal. Snakes and lizards are common and the range of bird life is great.

Fish in the coastal waters include rock cod weighing 500 pounds, sailfish of 100 pounds and horse mackerel weighing 80 pounds. Insects, extremely numerous, include several species of the tsetse fly, whose bite causes serious diseases in livestock and people.

OLDUVAI GORGE

Travelling from Ngorongoro to Serengeti one passes through the Masai tribe's grazing area and into the gorge where Dr. Louis S. B. Leakey and his wife Mary unearthed the remains of men thought to be 2,300,000 years old, perhaps the very beginnings of mankind.

Kilwa, a great 12th-century port which may have been known once as Quiloa, is today a haven for dhows sailing the coast of East Africa. The Kilwa region shows a great potential for archeological exploration. The ruins of this great Arab mosque can be visited today, along with other extensive Portuguese and Arab ruins.

2. HISTORY

FOR MANY CENTURIES, Western man held the view that Africa had no history, that the continent was isolated until the coming of the white missionaries and explorers early in the 19th century. Today, we no longer accept this myth because of archeological discoveries of Louis Leakey, the discovery and translation of Arab and Greek writings, and the study of linguistics and serology (study of blood types). Historians are replacing the myth with facts.

Although the entire story is not yet known, it is obvious that Tanzania has played a major rôle in the history of the continent.

The history of Tanzania had two distinct stages—the discovery and settlement of the coastal region and the island of Zanzibar, followed by the exploration and development by Europeans of the interior of what has historically been called Tanganyika. The entire coastal region of East Africa has been

Objects from the past in the Zanzibar Museum serve as a reminder of the Arab influence on the history of the island.

known and explored for over 2,000 years. In contrast, the interior of Tanganyika has only been discovered in the last century.

Perhaps the true beginning of Tanzania's history was discovered by the Leakeys at Olduvai Gorge, in northern Tanzania, between 1960 and 1963. Some fragments of skull, bone and tools that the Leakeys found were scientifically dated as 2,300,000 years old—the oldest remains ever classified as man. The skull had jaws and teeth which were adapted to eat both meat and fruit. There were some tools found near the skull and this is why scientists have classified him as a man. Other fossils and

Kondoa, in Central Province, is noted for its rock paintings from the Stone Age. It is not known who made these dark red paintings of animals and a hunting scene.

21

remains have been found in or near Tanzania but none can be classified as man. As a result of the Leakeys discoveries, Africa (and Tanzania particularly) is now considered the original home of man.

Although historians have not yet pieced the whole story of the early Africans together, they have proven that the Hamites entered what is today Tanzania from the Nile Valley in Egypt and the Sudan. These brown-skinned people migrated throughout East Africa during the Stone Age. It is believed that these Hamites met and mixed with a Negroid type of people during their migrations and the result was the birth of the Bantu people, East Africa's dominant group today. The Bantu were basically agricultural people and had little or no contact with the rest of the world until about A.D. 1000.

By that time, Arabs from the Persian Gulf area had founded a great empire along the coast of Tanzania. For centuries, Arab traders had contact with the Tanzanian coast as their boats were carried by the monsoon winds toward East Africa. The Arab empire was called Zinj, the Persian word for "black," and referred to the fact that the natives in the area were black-skinned. Great trade towns such as Kilwa, along the southern coast of Tanzania, and Bagamoyo,

about 45 miles north of where Dar es Salaam is today, were established and for five centuries the Arabs were dominant along the coast. The Arabs did not show much interest in exploring the interior, as they were content to trade for ivory, and later, slaves.

THE PORTUGUESE

At the end of the 15th century, a new force came upon the scene—the Portuguese began to show interest in East Africa. This was a result of the travels of Vasco da Gama, who sailed from Portugal round the southern tip of Africa to India. Da Gama's trip was begun in 1497 and the following year he sailed along the East African coast. He observed the prosperous Arab settlements with great interest, and his reports caused much excitement back in Portugal. Jealousy, greed for gold and ivory, and the prospects of more slaves, motivated Portugal to conquer the East African coast and drive the Arabs away. Very few Portuguese actually settled along the coast, but their ships raided the coastal trading posts. For 200 years, the Portuguese were in command. By 1698, however, the Arabs, with the help of the Turks, were able to drive the Portuguese out with a series of counter-attacks, and once more the Tanzanian coast came under Arab domination. Although some trading posts were destroyed as a result of the conflict between the Arabs and the Portuguese, many of them were rebuilt and were soon thriving again.

THE 18TH AND 19TH CENTURIES

After the Arabs had re-established control over the coast of East Africa at the end of the 17th century, the Arab pattern of trading and slavery returned. About the only change of importance in Arab policy came in 1832 when the capital of the Arab empire was moved from Muscat, on the Arabian Peninsula, to the island of Zanzibar. The ruler of the Arabs, Seyyid Said, was courted by the British, who hoped to get him to outlaw slavery along the East African coast. He did enter into some minor agreements, but the slave trade continued to thrive. Said died in 1856 and his Sultanate (empire) was divided between his sons. One son returned to Muscat to control the holdings in Arabia, while the other son remained in Zanzibar controlling East African lands. By 1873, the British were able to convince the Sultan of Zanzibar to outlaw slavery or suffer the consequences of naval bombardment.

MISSIONARY ACTIVITY

In the 1840's the first groups of missionaries arrived in East Africa, determined to Christianize the natives. Their zeal was often lessened by the extremely harsh terrain of the area and by rampant disease. Those missionaries who did survive set up missions in densely populated areas and concentrated their efforts on converting the tribal chiefs. With the chiefs in the fold, conversion of the masses would be much easier. Many missionaries emphasized schools as their method to conversion, which proved very popular with the Africans, and by the 1870's the missionary movement was in full progress. It was through the missionaries that the African learned about Europe and the European learned about the African. The missionary movement not only served to bring Christianity to the people of Africa, but helped to end the slave trade and to bring education and improved health to the region.

EXPLORING THE INTERIOR

European missionary activity in East Africa stimulated interest in the interior regions. During the 19th century, geographic interest in the whole continent of Africa took hold in Europe, and in the next century, while it lasted, East Africa was opened up. As a rule, the men interested in exploring the interior were motivated by scientific and humanitarian reasons.

The first great explorers of East Africa, two German Christian Missionary Society members, named Rebmann and Krapf, are credited with being the first Europeans to see Mount Kili-

This shore line view of Zanzibar town looks on the whitewashed stone structures housing export-import offices. Zanzibar town, over 300 years old, is the seat of the island's government. There is an old saying that when the drums beat on Zanzibar the people dance on the mainland. This emphasizes the importance of Zanzibar's rôle in the history and development of East Africa.

manjaro in Tanzania. These two men made their exploration between 1847 and 1849, and their journey was a great achievement because they took a long and hazardous route through southern Kenya, and the lands of the warlike Masai. Later explorations in East Africa followed a more southerly route through Tanganyika, which was easier and safer.

The next important step in the exploration of Tanganyika occurred in the 1850's and 1860's when David Livingstone, an English antislavery missionary, made various explorations into East Africa from his South African base. Livingstone had explored first mainly in West Africa. He wrote accounts of his trips which aroused great interest in England. Two British explorers named Richard Burton and J. H. Speke meanwhile discovered Lake Tanganyika, Africa's second largest lake.

Later, Speke and James Grant explored the area around Lake Victoria and the River Nile in Uganda. While Livingstone was exploring the lands that are today southern Tanzania, he

native chiefs. These treaties, whose legality was doubtful, became the basis for German claims in Tanganyika as Europe prepared for the quick partitioning of the continent in the last decade of the 19th century.

GERMAN INVOLVEMENT

As a result of agreements made with England, France and Belgium in 1886 and 1890, Germany gained a colonial foothold in Tanganyika and Ruanda-Urundi (now Rwanda and Burundi). At these conferences, rules were established for colonization and claims were laid out. This partitioning of Africa had profound effects on Tanganyika. Lake Victoria served as the geographic basis for the partition. Land to the north of the middle of the lake was to be British and land to the south was to be the property of Germany.

While the Germans were aggressive in the negotiations, the British, as a result of their experience in the colonial market, were passive. The only time England did make demands was when their right to Uganda was questioned by the Germans. England, wanting to control Uganda and the source of the River Nile, would not back down, and Germany had to be content with its holdings in Tanganyika.

At first, the German government attempted to have Tanganyika administered by a private company called the German East Africa Company. This arrangement failed as the administrators proved to be very harsh rulers. They often ran afoul of the natives with their policies on ownership of land and forced work rules. Finally, in 1891, the German government had no choice but to take over the colonial administration. Although government officials did not prove to be any more skillful in administering the colony, they did have military

discovered Lake Nyasa. His reports of his daring adventures made him rich and famous, in the United States as well as in Britain. On his last journey he started out from Zanzibar toward Bagamoyo, to cross Tanganyika to the Congo. During this long and dangerous trek, Livingstone disappeared and was not heard from for five years. The newspaper-reading public feared the worst, and a New York reporter, Henry M. Stanley, was dispatched to find the missing missionary-explorer and send back reports. On November 10, 1871 Stanley finally found his man at the village of Ujiji, on Lake Tanganyika. Stanley's greeting became famous: "Dr. Livingstone, I presume."

With new maps and data concerning the lands of East Africa, the European powers finally had enough interest and information to begin colonization. The British started the Imperial British East Africa Company. Germany became involved largely through the efforts of Dr. Karl Peters who, in 1884, made a whirlwind six-week journey through the interior of Tanganyika and signed a dozen treaties with power at their command. Revolts by the Arabs along the coast and by Africans in southern Tanganyika were suppressed.

The most famous and largest uprising of Tanganyikans, the "Maji-Maji" revolt in 1905, was caused by Germany's forced work policy. It affected the southern half of Tanganyika and lasted for two years. The cost in lives has been estimated at 100,000. Hundreds of villages were burned by the Germans in an attempt to put down the insurrection. The effect of the "Maji-Maji" revolt was that many beneficial economic and educational reforms followed.

In the years that Germany stayed in East Africa, the colonies in that area were failing economically. Germany was getting very little out of Tanganyika, especially considering the frustrations of dealing with numerous revolts, and the necessary economic reforms. Sisal, a plant whose fibre can be used for cord and rope, was introduced into Tanganyika at a very great expense by the Germans. The climate seemed ideal for growing sisal and it was believed that a great industry could be developed. Coffee, too, was introduced for much the same reasons. Railway construction was begun as the Germans noted the success the British were having with railways in Uganda and Kenya. The German colonial officials also attempted to build a cotton industry.

To get Tanganyika to yield a profit, the Germans never abolished slavery, fearing that ending it would have a bad effect on Tanganyika's economy.

WORLD WAR I AND ITS AFTERMATH

While war was raging in Europe from 1914 through 1918, none of the nations involved in it were much concerned with East Africa. The climate and terrain of Kenya, Uganda and Tanganyika were not suited to moving troops and digging trenches. If England had its way, the war would never have reached East Africa. Germany, on the other hand, followed a strategy of threatening British African territories without fighting. Therefore, little happened as a direct result of the war. The main results came after Germany and its allies were defeated.

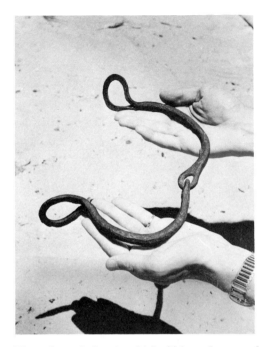

These slave chains, in which African slaves used to be bound by their Arab masters, can still be seen in a museum in Bagamoyo. Also at the museum there is a large, old baobab tree in which a shackle ring for holding slaves remains embedded.

In 1919, after the long peace conferences, the victorious powers broke up the German colonial empire. Germany had to give up its holdings as the penalty for waging and losing the war. Germany's West African holdings were split between France and England. Its southwest African colonies were awarded to the Union of South Africa. East Africa, however, presented a problem. The British were not very excited about Tanganyika and Ruanda-Urundi. They asked Italy to take these lands, but the Italians refused. Woodrow Wilson, the U.S. president, refused Tanganyika when it was offered to him. Finally, a compromise was worked out whereby Tanganyika became a League of Nations "B" mandate.

There were two types of mandates evolved by the League of Nations. Under an "A" mandate, the country involved would soon be granted full independence. Under a "B" mandate, the country was considered in no way ready for

Dar es Salaam appeared as a sleepy seaport in 1903 but later replaced Bagamoyo as Tanganyika's main port. The narrow entrance to the port was widened and deepwater berths added in 1956.

independence for quite some time. Tanganyika, with its poor economy and backward peoples, was designated a "B" mandate.

It was the hope of the members of the League of Nations that Tanganyika would be protected from slavery, forced work and other abuses. Great Britain was placed in charge of the mandate and, as administering authority, was to submit an annual report about events to the members of the League. Many authorities believe England intended to join Tanganyika eventually with Kenya and Uganda, their profitable colonies nearby.

Britain held the mandate on Tanganyika from 1922 to after World War II. In this period, Tanganyika's people were ruled more indirectly than under the German style of rule. For example, under the Germans, districts were assigned to a German officer. Sub-districts were ruled by officials called akidas who had chiefs under them. The akidas were often Arabs and were just as different from the natives they ruled as were the Germans. The akidas took all problems to the German who ruled directly over them.

Under the British mandate, rule was placed in the hands of the local native administrations. Some rights and responsibilities were given to tribal leaders, but the ultimate power rested with the British. This form of government made communication easier and more meaningful to the Africans. The local chiefs maintained law and order, made some local laws and collected taxes.

TANGANYIKA AS A U.N. TRUSTEESHIP

While much of the world was ravaged by World War II, Tanganyika remained quiet, but the effects of the war on Tanganyika were felt. Many of the officials in charge of the mandate had to be recalled to England, for they were needed in the war effort. This left much of the power in the hands of the tribal chiefs. In addition, some Tanganyikans were drafted and sent to fight in Europe. After the war, many of these men returned with a different outlook. The chiefs, too, had tasted power while the administrative officials were away. These two factors were to play a great rôle in the quest for independence in the next two decades. These young Tanganyikans who were asked to fight in Europe for freedom against tyranny, upon arriving home in Tanganyika, wanted the same kind of freedom.

After World War II, Tanganyika became a United Nations trusteeship under the supervision of England. This differed from the man-

In 1964, Julius Nyerere visited Communist China and there he met Chairman Mao Tse-tung. Nyerere observed the socialist life in China and got some ideas for his own nation. Israel, too, with its "kibbutz" system has also had an effect on the President's thinking.

date in that it encouraged the development of political institutions in Tanganyika, and the people could become more directly involved in the administration of their own country. The end result would be eventual self-government or independence. To ensure that the trusteeship was working towards this goal, the United Nations sent visiting missions to Tanganyika every three years to serve as fact-finding bodies. They studied government documents and interviewed the Tanganyikans.

Paralleling the trusteeship came the birth and development of the Tanganyikan African National Union (TANU), the first native political party to have popular support. TANU provided the United Nations missions with a true voice of the people to balance the voice of the administrating authority. Some historians feel that Tanganyika's strong native political party prevented white settler domination of Tanganyika—unlike what happened in Rhodesia, where white settlers kept complete control. The growth of TANU was also aided by the general disapproval of colonialism in the United Nations.

Britain, too, had seen the handwriting on the wall. Independence had already been granted to India, and gradual release of all colonies was planned, but East Africa's future was not clear. First there would have to be a strengthening of traditional tribal governments at the local level and in time the creation of a national assembly of native Africans. As late as 1955, only four Africans sat on the Legislative Council. Four times as many Europeans were council members. Even if there had been an African majority on the council, the Legislative Council was merely an advisory body, as the terms of the trusteeship still placed the power in the hands of the British Governor of Tanganyika.

JULIUS NYERERE AND TANU

Before TANU there had been the Tanganyikan African Civil Service Union of the 1920's. This group, comprised mostly of government (colonial) workers and teachers, did not display much influence or solidarity. The next attempt at national parties came in 1929 in the form of the Tanganyikan African Association (TAA), an inter-tribal group, composed mainly of educated Africans. However, this group did not capture much public support and for 24 years had little effect on events in Tanganyika.

But, in 1953 the TAA elected Julius Nyerere as its president and he set about to reform the organization. Under his leadership a new constitution for the party was drafted and its name changed to TANU. He hoped to gain recognition for the party among the masses, not just the small educated élite. The goal of TANU also included agricultural reforms and free elections.

Born in 1922, Julius Nyerere was educated in Catholic schools and earned a degree from Makerere College in Uganda. One of the few Tanganyikans chosen to study abroad, he

27

political purposes. TANU was outlawed in certain districts as a threat to law and order. All of these steps, however, were overcome by the party with the help of the trade unionists and the United Nations Mission. TANU still held meetings, at times secretly in the forests, and literature was passed around the country, despite the ban on the party. Oscar Kambona, the full-time general secretary of TANU, found time while studying in England to begin a publicity campaign depicting the Tanganyikan's plight in his own country. Not long afterwards, the British Parliament began to discuss the problems of the trusteeship.

Nyerere and the leaders of TANU decided to take their case to the U.N. Mission in charge of Tanganyika in 1954. Through a written memorandum, TANU outlined its position on the problems and future of Tanganyika. The party brought to the attention of the mission the poverty of the people and the lack of schools in the trusteeship. They argued against any plan to make Tanganyika a part of an East African federation dominated by white settlers. Also, TANU asked for a more racially balanced representation on the Legislative Council.

The United Nations Visiting Mission, after studying the situation, in its report to the Trusteeship Council proposed a schedule for independence by 1979. Tanganyika's colonial administration retaliated by down-playing TANU's importance. To maintain the support of the U.N. Mission, Julius Nyerere flew to New York to bring the plight of the Tanganyikans before the world body. By demanding free elections and increased African participation in the government of the trusteeship, Nyerere impressed many U.N. members with his multi-racial policies. He promised full citizenship and participation for Asians and Europeans living in Tanganyika.

earned his master's degree from the University of Edinburgh in Scotland and on his return was assigned as a teacher at Tabora.

The growth of TANU is indeed amazing when one considers how conditions in Tanganyika worked against the party. The country is geographically large and transportation and communication were non-existent in many parts of it. The people of Tanganyika had little education or experience in political organization. Working against TANU was the colonial administration, which tried to prevent the people from learning about and joining the party. Despite these huge obstacles, the TANU party slowly gained in strength.

The British authorities in Tanganyika started their own campaign in the mid-1950's against TANU and its leaders. The British were attempting to encourage tribal associations rather than a unified national association. Chiefs were bribed to tell their people that TANU was bad for the country. Licenses for public meetings and rallies sponsored by TANU were not issued by the administering authority. There was discrimination in government hiring of those active in the party. Julius Nyerere was not allowed to travel outside certain areas for

President Julius Nyerere and a crowd of onlookers obviously are enjoying the amusing dance being performed by an old woman. The music is provided by a "zeze," a traditional harp-like instrument made from a wooden bowl and goat-skin.

Nyerere made numerous visits to New York in 1955 and 1956, and the name of Tanganyika became familiar to the member nations. Because there was so much to be done at home, Nyerere next concentrated on developments taking place in Tanganyika. The colonial government, in an attempt to cut down on TANU's popularity, began sponsoring the United Tanganyika Party, which stood for the things the colonial administration stood for. It stated that until independence, Tanganyika was the responsibility of Britain, not the United Nations, and urged the people to respect the colonial authority.

The challenge of the UTP never amounted to much, because at its height in 1958 the party only had 10,000 members. TANU, on the other hand, could count on support from its 250,000 members. In the elections of 1958-59, TANU showed its power by sweeping five provinces, and a year later, by winning a dozen more seats on the Legislative Council. During the election, Julius Nyerere was prosecuted for libel and found guilty. He had to pay a fine, but he was shrewd enough to publicize his case in order to gain sympathy. Many people believe the fine actually helped his party's candidates to their overwhelming victory. After the elections of 1958-59, the UTP disbanded, as it became obvious that TANU had the support of the people.

EVENTS LEADING TO INDEPENDENCE

With the growth of TANU as a political power came a change in the top leadership of the trusteeship. The new Governor of Tanganyika, Sir Richard Turnbull, had been chief secretary in Kenya during the bloody "Mau Mau" emergency in that colony during the early and middle 1950's. His experience with violence in Kenya made him resolve to prevent a similar happening in Tanganyika. Julius Nyerere welcomed Turnbull's appointment to Tanganyika as he felt that the colonial administration would be more liberal towards TANU and its quest for self-government.

Political conditions improved after the elections of 1958-59. Reports from the provinces told of TANU members helping the colonial administration in tax collections. The hope of independence caused TANU members to co-operate with the colonial authority, relieve tensions and generally support administration moves. By late 1959, Nyerere was predicting independence within five years. Governor Turnbull touched off great anticipation and excitement when he announced in December, 1959, that Tanganyika would have some sort of responsible government the following year.

The last U.N. mission came to Tanganyika in 1960 and, after exchanging memoranda with the colonial authorities and Julius Nyerere for TANU, it reported that the country was due for independence as early as possible. The only problems the report stressed were economic ones, as the people of Tanganyika were quite poor. The report commended the native peoples for their patience and good will.

To celebrate independence in 1961, a symbolic torch of freedom was placed at the top of Mount Kilimanjaro. President Nyerere referred to the torch as a beacon to be seen by all who view Africa's highest mountain. Tanzania's flag has a green triangle in its upper left-hand corner and a blue triangle in its lower right-hand corner, separated by a black stripe with gold bands.

SELF-GOVERNMENT AND INDEPENDENCE

Self-government was granted to Tanganyika on May 1, 1961, and independence was planned later in the year, in December. Tanganyikans began to supervise their own affairs under the guidance of the Governor, who still had the power to make decisions affecting foreign affairs and defence. Full independence meant that Tanganyika was freed from colonial administration entirely. Julius Nyerere became the Prime Minister. The Legislative Council, historic symbol of colonial rule, was replaced by a National Assembly. Tanganyika applied after all for membership in the Commonwealth of Nations and Britain worked for its acceptance. In the seven months preceding independence, Tanganyika received close to US $500,000,000 in offers of aid from Britain, the U.S. and Germany. Other financing was sought from France, the Scandinavian countries and the U.N.

After TANU won another election in 1960, Governor Turnbull met with Julius Nyerere to request that he form a government. The Governor suggested a constitutional conference in London, to be held in March, 1961. This made the independence movement an accepted fact. But work and planning remained. Julius Nyerere now travelled to Britain, Germany and the United States to try to gain financial pledges to assist Tanganyikan development.

It was also at this time Nyerere became a spokesman against the South African apartheid (separatist) régime. Nyerere was firm in his position against racism. He warned Britain that when independence came, Tanganyika would refuse to join the British Commonwealth of Nations, the economic union under which former colonies had trade privileges. This was a unique position, for Nyerere was risking future British aid with this threat.

To strengthen his position, Nyerere appealed to the independent nations of West Africa to boycott all goods from South Africa until the apartheid policies were dropped. This attack on South Africa's policies may have had some effect on that nation's quitting Britain's Commonwealth of Nations. Nyerere's image as an African statesman of integrity grew.

Prime Minister Nyerere encouraged the European settlers to stay and work in independent Tanganyika. He did not want these trained people to panic and leave the new nation with severe manpower shortages. He assured colonial government workers by letters and speeches that they would not be replaced by Africans (although that was the announced policy and goal of the government) until they retired or left of their own choice. In addition, in October, 1961, these workers were given wage increases.

The new constitution guaranteed individual rights, universal adult suffrage, and impartial law courts. Any person born in Tanganyika with one parent also born there would be a citizen when independence came. After independence, any person born in Tanganyika would automatically be a citizen.

Julius Nyerere (far right), on December 9, 1961, appears pensive at the Independence Day celebrations in Dar es Salaam.

On December 9, 1961, independence was formally granted to Tanganyika by Britain, represented in person by the Duke of Edinburgh. To house the Independence Day celebrations, the National Assembly authorized the building of a National Stadium in Dar es Salaam. Parades and parties highlighted the day. In his speeches during the week before Independence Day, Julius Nyerere warned the people that independence would not bring rapid economic change. He predicted a long, slow and difficult process for Tanganyika to develop economic stability.

UNION BETWEEN TANGANYIKA AND ZANZIBAR

The governments of the world were quite surprised in 1964 when it was announced that huge Tanganyika and the tiny island of Zanzibar had joined together to form the Republic of Tanzania. To those who knew East African history best, the union was probably no shock, as historically the Sultans of Zanzibar had great power and interest on the mainland. During the colonial period, from 1890 on, the power of the Sultans on the mainland had greatly diminished, although the historical roots could not be erased.

Zanzibar, with its people divided into various associations along racial lines, had had a stormy road to independence. This was in direct contrast to the relatively peaceful independence movement in mainland Tanganyika. The majority group on the island of Zanzibar were the Shirazis, African descendants of the Persians who had come to Zanzibar in the 10th century. Zanzibar's second largest group were the Africans of mainland ancestry. The most powerful group on the island were the Arabs who were urbanized and affluent. In addition there was a small Indian community. Each group distrusted the other, especially the Shirazis and the Arabs. The native Africans resented both the Arabs and the Shirazis, and the three were unanimous in their distrust of the Indian group.

Yet, despite the rivalries between these groups, Zanzibar gained its independence from Britain on December 10, 1963. Independence did not solve the tiny island's problems, however, and 13 months afterwards the island was the scene of a violent "coup d'état" in which Sultan Seyyid Khalifa was overthrown by the Afro-Shirazi coalition party. Abeid Amani Karume became the leader of Zanzibar. He and Julius Nyerere, after many discussions, produced the union between the island and the mainland.

The new republic had Nyerere as its President

These traditional dancers from the Lake Victoria region travelled well over 700 miles to the capital, Dar es Salaam, to celebrate the arrival of Sekou Toure, the president of the Republic of Guinea. Occasions of national importance are usually marked by traditional dancing.

and Karume as First Vice-President. The National Assembly was expanded to include a large Zanzibari representation and the official name was changed to Tanzania, a combination of the names Tanganyika and Zanzibar. The central government of the new republic remained at Dar es Salaam and is responsible for defence, foreign affairs and public services.

Food and agriculture is the theme of this new 5-shilling piece.

The once sleepy town of Arusha gained international attention in February, 1967, when President Julius Nyerere announced there the form of African Socialism to be followed in Tanzania's future. The town gained further importance the following year when the three leaders of the East African nations met there to reorganize the East African Common Services Organization and agreed on Arusha as permanent headquarters.

3. GOVERNMENT AND SOCIAL SERVICES

THE UNITED REPUBLIC of Tanzania has a president and two vice-presidents as heads of state. The president is elected by the voters and he in turn selects his two vice-presidents from the elected members of the National Assembly. The second vice-president's duties include serving as head of the National Assembly. Tanzania is a unicameral republic—that is, it has only one law-making body, the National Assembly, with 204 members. Approximately one-fourth of the Assembly seats are reserved for representatives from Zanzibar.

On the regional level, mainland Tanzania is divided into 17 provinces, each governed by a regional commissioner. The islands of Zanzibar and Pemba are divided into three regions administratively. These regional commissioners are appointed by the central

The "Ujamaa" (togetherness) policy is evident in the Shinyanga region, near Lake Victoria in northwestern Tanzania. School children give a helping hand in making bricks for a new hospital building.

Rural Tanzania relies heavily on radio broadcasts for the daily news, but lack of electricity necessitates the use of battery-powered radios. These men have been given this radio as a reward for their work in an "Ujamaa" or co-operative village.

government to oversee the activities in each region. Assistant regional commissioners and district commissioners aid the regional commissioners on the local level. Even small villages have weekly meetings, called *barazas*, to deal with local problems. The *barazas* are traditional in African democracy.

PHILOSOPHY OF THE GOVERNMENT

The government of Tanzania is committed to a policy of African Socialism, which can be defined as a large-scale attempt to capture tribal co-operation of the past on the national level. The goal of African Socialism is economic in nature. The hope is that through co-operative agricultural production, income will improve. African Socialism stresses sharing and equality. The motto of this movement in Tanzania is *Ujamaa,* a Swahili word which means "togetherness" or "familyhood." By sticking together, the people of Tanzania would be similar to one large extended family. In a way, the *Ujamaa* villages springing up through Tanzania resemble the *kibbutz* communities of Israel. President Nyerere has been the spearhead of the *Ujamaa* concept. This idea of self-sacrifice and unity is implemented by government officials who happily receive small salaries for long hours of service. President Nyerere himself lives modestly with his wife and eight children in Dar es Salaam.

ONE-PARTY SYSTEM

The African concept of democracy is similar to that of the ancient Greeks, from whom we have received the word "democracy." To the Greeks, democracy meant "government by discussion among equals." The people of Greece discussed their affairs until they reached a consensus or general agreement. The decision therefore was a "people's decision." Talking until agreement is reached is at the heart of traditional African democracy. Democracy as practiced in Europe and America places great emphasis on majority vote and/or organized opposition through various political parties.

1738170

Although countries as large as Tanzania cannot practice the "pure" democracy of the ancient Greeks, an attempt has been made through a one-party system to facilitate discussion. Dissent is allowed in the party discussions, but after the discussions decisions are announced as unified. President Nyerere has summed up the position of the one-party state by explaining: "In Western democracies it is an accepted practice in times of emergency for opposition parties to sink their differences and join together in forming a national government. This is our time of emergency, and until our war against poverty, ignorance and disease has been won, we should not let our unity be destroyed by a desire to follow somebody else's book of rules."

NATIONALIZATION POLICIES

In 1967, the Tanzanian government nationalized (took control over) the banks of Tanzania, in addition to all trading, insurance and food-processing companies. The justification for this move was that it equalized economic power between public and private owners. Most of the nationalized industries were owned and operated by non-Africans, either Asians or Europeans. Nyerere and other leaders hoped that the

35

In a speech before a huge throng, President Julius Nyerere announced his policy of self-reliance. He stated "TANU is involved in a war against poverty and oppression in our country; this struggle is aimed at moving the people of Tanzania (and the people of Africa as a whole) from a state of poverty to a state of prosperity. We have been oppressed a great deal, we have been exploited a great deal and we have been disregarded a great deal. It is our weakness that has led to our being oppressed, exploited, and disregarded. We now intend to bring about a revolution which will ensure that we are never again victims of these things."

nationalization would speed up economic development. While the world had mixed reactions to the move, Nyerere immediately made agreements with the private companies which remained unnationalized. Today, many foreign companies are operating in partnership with the government of Tanzania.

NEUTRALITY, NATIONALISM AND PAN-AFRICANISM

In foreign policy, Tanzania is committed to a policy of neutrality between East and West. President Nyerere and his government have encouraged Britain and the United States to help Tanzania. Aid is also sought and accepted from the Soviet Union and Communist China. Nyerere has evidently succeeded in this non-alignment policy as he has often been criticized by both camps for being too friendly with the other side.

Tanzania's government is a leading spokesman on affairs of the continent. Attempts have been made to launch propaganda campaigns against colonialism in Rhodesia, Mozambique, and South Africa. Exiles from these white-ruled nations are welcomed in Tanzania and many liberation organizations have their offices in

Tanzania's railways are operated by the East African Common Services Organization. Once the railways were separated by national boundaries, but now service is integrated throughout Tanzania, Kenya, and Uganda.

Dar es Salaam. Liberation armies have been given the use of land in southern Tanzania as training ground. The Nyerere government is thus exemplifying the spirit of Pan-Africanism.

Tanzania is a leading member in the Organization for African Unity, which brings together the independent nations of Africa.

Self-reliance is Tanzania's policy and these people use their hands to make a new road near their homes.

This mass demonstration in support of the Arusha Declaration took place in Dar es Salaam in 1967, and placards in support of the government's future policies were widely displayed. Nyerere was elected for another term in 1970 with 97 per cent of the voters approving.

EAST AFRICAN CO-OPERATION

Building on the historical free trade agreement made by Britain in 1923, the East African nations have entered into an elaborate economic union. The union, declared in 1967, was jointly announced by Julius Nyerere, Milton Obote of Uganda, and Jomo Kenyatta of Kenya. The three countries of East Africa, with a combined population of over 30,000,000, contribute equally to maintain the capital of the East African Community at Arusha in Tanzania. A new headquarters for the union will be housed in Arusha, which lies at the geographic center of East Africa.

The union participates in such activities as trade and industrial development, banking, research, transportation and communication. It operates four financially independent corporations: East African Harbours, East African Railways, East African Posts and Telecommunications, and East African Airways. Taxes and customs are also collected jointly. Besides, the community is working together on various phases of research including forestry, agriculture, marine fisheries and tropical diseases.

Tanzania's government has been aggressive in bringing the East African Community into being, and Julius Nyerere has even envisioned a political union some day between Kenya, Uganda and Tanzania, but nationalistic pride would have to be put aside.

Nutrition is an important concern of the schools. Here a government inspector explains how to prepare food without damaging the nutritional value.

HEALTH AND EDUCATION

Tanzania is not a healthy country, as evidenced by its individual life expectancy of 38 years. More than 90 per cent of the Tanzanians live in rural areas where medical facilities are limited and modern health habits unknown. Historically, health information was

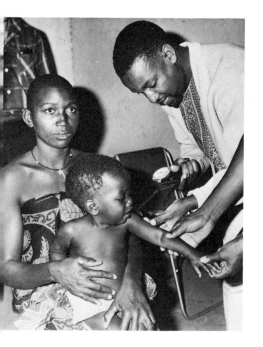

given by parents in the tribes to their children (much of which was erroneous), stories were told with health morals, and health was the province of witch doctors and medicine men. When the missionaries came and settled in Tanzania and other parts of East Africa, they pointed out the diseases and the people understood. Immunization was begun to prevent disease.

Today, the government of Tanzania is stressing curative medicine more than preventive medicine, because its prevention projects are very expensive and require mass education. It is doing its best to build hospitals and clinics for people in the remote areas. Medicines are being supplied for the major diseases—malnutrition, tuberculosis, malaria, dysentery, schistosomiasis, elephantiasis, smallpox, typhoid and sleeping sickness. The government is striving to train more physicians (now one doctor for every 21,000 people) and provide more than one hospital bed for every 569 people.

Infant mortality has long been a problem in Tanzania. Diet deficiencies, usually a lack of protein, are common causes of disease and deformities. By making public health services free, the government of Tanzania hopes to eradicate these diseases arising from poor nutrition.

39

Overcrowding and lack of supplies are still serious problems in Tanzania's schools, especially in rural areas. Yet, despite these obstacles, primary education standards have risen since Independence.

These children in a nursery school are learning as they play.

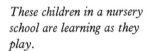

Physical fitness is an important part of education in Tanzania.

These youngsters are studying hard—primary education in Tanzania is a serious matter because parents must pay school fees to send their children to school.

In a nation where the per capita annual income is around US $73, education is extremely important. Julius Nyerere was the first Tanzanian to become a university graduate, and it was natural for his government to support education heavily. Tanzania can boast of a fine university at Dar es Salaam. This modern institution of higher learning was at one time affiliated with the University of East Africa (including University College, Nairobi and Makerere College in Uganda), but at present the university is separate with its own curriculum. Over a dozen teachers' colleges are located in Tanzania and there are many secondary and technical schools. All of the schools are under the supervision of the

Reading lessons get the undivided attention of these girls from the coast of Tanzania. They are dressed in picturesque "kangas," which are attractive in appearance as well as a protection from the equatorial sun.

41

Tanzania requires a period of service to the nation from its young people. These women, members of the National Service, are parading to show their loyalty to President Nyerere and the government. The ladies are carrying "pangas," an all-purpose garden tool, to symbolize their efforts in clearing land.

Ministry of Education, which sets standards, curricula and educational policy. Primary schools offer 7 years of education, including instruction in history, geography, mathematics, health education, physical education, science, Swahili and English.

Students at the Mtwara Girls' Secondary School clear a site for their school garden. The implement they are using is called a "jembe" and is similar to a hoe.

Primary school children are required to learn about agriculture in addition to other studies. These boys are tending papaya trees at Korogwe in the Tanga region.

Modern school buildings of stone and tile are replacing the mud huts formerly used. Glass windows have replaced openings in the walls and children now have better lighting for their studies.

The back of a truck serves as a portable classroom for this adult education instructor. Literacy is highest along the coast, and the government is attempting to raise the literacy rate inland.

This group of Wanyakyusa tribesmen are in a festive mood for a harvest celebration. The dancers wave their fly whisks as the chief looks on with interest. In the background are long-leafed banana trees.

4. PEOPLE

THE COASTAL COUNTRIES of Africa are the home of many interesting cultural groups—about 120 tribes of Africans are indigenous to the mainland of Tanzania alone. In 1966, Tanzania was estimated to contain 13,000,000 people, including 116,000 Asians and 20,000 Europeans. This compares with a 9,000,000 population in Uganda and 11,000,000 in Kenya, both of which are much smaller in area.

The immigration to mainland Tanganyika from Asia began when employees were needed to build the railway to Uganda at the beginning

of the 20th century. In recent years Asians have held the positions of merchants, technicians, and money managers. Arabians had been residents of Zanzibar and the other islands and coastal towns for many centuries. Some Asians who chose not to adopt Tanzanian citizenship in 1961 have been leaving the country. Those remaining have visibly retained the cultural traditions of their homelands—India, Pakistan, and Arabia.

Thousands of Europeans came to Tanzania during the first half of the 20th century to

An elder of the Sambaa tribe of northeastern Tanzania puffs thoughtfully on his pipe. Meerschaum pipes of high quality are manufactured at Arusha. The features of this man show distinct Arab characteristics.

settle on fertile lands and to create a culture of their own. Since independence in 1961, a new rôle for the European has been developing. While many elected to become citizens of the new country, many others returned to their homelands and the countries of their ancestors.

The U.S. and Western European governments, realizing the needs of the new nation, have, through their foreign aid projects, sent many volunteers and short-term contract employees to spend a few years as teachers, doctors, and technicians to help in Tanzania's development.

AFRICANS

The many small tribes and many languages of Tanzania make studying the natives very different from studying the African people of

Kenya where there are only two large and dominant tribes. Of Tanzania's 120 tribes nearly all are of Bantu origin. Intermarriage between tribes is common, and inter-tribe rivalry is not a serious problem. Chiefdoms are the form of local government.

CENTRAL HIGHLAND PEOPLES

In the 141,000 square miles of the central highlands, called Unyamwezi, there are only 194 chiefdoms. In the Tabora region, as an example, the population has remained sparse but stable in spite of an increase in the country generally. Here the largest tribe is the Sukuma, and the other inhabitants are members of the Nyamwezi tribe. The population is sparse

The Masai of northern Tanzania are perhaps the most famous tribe of East Africa because they remain a pastoral people and resist pressures to change dress and customs. Tourists are especially fond of the Masai because photographs of them give an idea of life on the African continent hundreds of years ago. The government of Tanzania has requested that the Masai men wear trousers and shirts when travelling in towns like Arusha, rather than their loose-fitting blankets.

The central region of Tanzania is the home of the Wagogo tribe. These Wagogo girls are preparing the land for planting, using the hand hoe ("jembe"), the traditional farming implement of Tanzania.

Usually marriage is arranged by having the groom pay the bride's family a "bride price." The young couple will usually not live with the husband's family or clan, but family ties are important nevertheless. If a friend helps him build his new house he is in "debt," but if members of his own family come to help with the building there is no debt. Families gather to celebrate rituals of birth, marriage, death, and house building.

VILLAGE LIFE

In a town of several thousand people the population is mixed. A few Europeans may work in government offices or hospitals, and a few Asians may have shops or trucking businesses, but nearly all the people are African. Many claim to be Moslem, and a considerable number claim to be Christian. The proportion of the population practicing these religions depends upon their nearness to mosques and

because few rivers spring from the dry forests and there are many insect pests. Settlements consist of scattered villages of a few houses— a large village may have 100 houses.

A man's home may consist of one or more huts surrounded by a hedge. The clearing between the huts is used for work, play, and meals. Huts or houses are usually round, with mud walls and grass roofs. In this area it never freezes, and midday temperatures permit normal work habits. Because his house is paid for by taxes, the chief lives in a stone house with an iron roof, the style desired by most Africans.

FAMILY CUSTOMS

Many of the people of Unyamwezi have travelled. Many of them go to the coast for trade and jobs, sometimes staying a year or longer. In the countryside of Unyamwezi the language is that of the local tribe—Swahili is only used to talk to Asian merchants. Few men have more than two wives, and most men have only one.

This Nyaturu lady is wearing a head-dress made of sisal and beads. Her people live in the central highlands near Dodoma, about 300 miles inland from Dar es Salaam.

In sharp contrast, the traditional thatched roof exists side by side with a new corrugated iron roof. The government is encouraging the building of more new houses.

missions. Men outnumber women in the towns, but women may own most of the houses in the towns.

In smaller villages, Europeans and Asian shops are fewer, and there are fewer paved streets and walkways. Businesses here deal in essentials—lamp oil, corn grinding, clothing, and fuel for the buses and trucks in the area.

CITY LIFE

In the northernmost corner of the central highlands is the city of Arusha, capital of the East African Common Services Organization. The life of the growing city is often in contrast with the way of life of the Masai people (see back cover) who live in the countryside. Tourists often make Arusha their headquarters to safari into the well-known game parks and to climb Mt. Kilimanjaro. Tourism is encouraged by the government, and its bustle is added to the usual village life. In Arusha, one can see African game guides and their tourists leaving for safaris in their Land Rovers, Masai tribesmen in the city for shopping at the open-air markets, and African government officers in town for a meeting of the EACSO.

EASTERN TANZANIA PEOPLE

The people of this area are cultivators, iron workers, basket weavers, and carvers, and many families keep livestock. The housing and village

Traditionally in Tanzania, houses are built communally by the men in a village. The person building the house supplies food and drink for those who help him, and is expected to help them build their houses when the time comes.

Along the east coast of Tanzania, and on the islands of Zanzibar and Pemba, Arab influence can be seen on numerous elaborately carved doors. This door, located at Bagamoyo, displays the intricate patterns used for centuries. Local laws prohibit the removing or defacing of such doors on Zanzibar.

COASTAL PEOPLES

The Swahili-speaking people live in villages along the coast and on nearby islands, and represent a variety of racial and ethnic backgrounds. There are coastal Africans whose tribal customs and language are purely Swahili. One group is the Shirazi who claim to have intermarried with the Persian invaders between A.D. 900 and 1300. There are members of other tribes who came to the coast for a variety of

pattern is very similar to that found around Tabora. Along the coast near Pangani, land is scarce and land holdings are smaller than inland.

In the area of Mpwapwa the climate is dry and more nearly like that of the Tabora area. This area was well travelled by explorers during the early part of the 20th century, and the people have had considerable contact with Arabs. The tribes are small but numerous, and their languages are varied. Most of the chiefs at the time of independence owed their positions to the influence of Arabs or Europeans.

Homes here reflect Arab influence. Doorways are carved in the Arab fashion. Houses are frequently square, and the exterior is often plastered in white.

FAMILY CUSTOMS AND VILLAGE LIFE

The bride price in the Eastern area is lower than paid inland. Divorce can be obtained with the agreement of the unlucky couple's families. Often the bride price must be repaid in order for the divorce to be allowed.

Here the home and village residence patterns are more often based on kinship. As in most East African societies, there are special rites for birth, puberty, marriage, and death.

Tourists can find a wide variety of crafts in the streets of Dar. Carvers from all over East Africa send their wares to the cities for sale. Prices are flexible and are often arrived at after much haggling. Bargaining is carried out in a friendly manner, the general rule for tourists being to settle on half of the seller's original price.

Moslem ladies out for a walk pass an old Arab mosque in Zanzibar town. The Moslem ladies of Zanzibar and East Africa's coast appear in public in a "buibui," a black garment covering them from head to foot.

The Makonde tribe, in addition to their fame as East Africa's finest carvers, are creative dancers. Here, at a celebration, stilt dancers perform in fanciful costumes.

reasons and stayed long enough to accept the Swahili language.

In addition to Indians living in this area there are numerous Arabs. Their home countries have maintained trade with coastal Africa for many centuries—predating Vasco da Gama and even Marco Polo.

VILLAGE LIFE

Marriage along the coast is less stable, and tribal customs have less influence there than inland. Swahili is replacing the tribal languages.

Unlike the people in inland towns and villages, coastal peoples do not move with changes of season or rainfall. Their buildings are made of more permanent materials. On the islands of Zanzibar and Pemba, streets are narrow, and central business sections are quite Arabian in style. Schools are more plentiful here, and the literacy rate is high.

CITY LIFE

The variety of races and modes of dress found in Dar, Tanga, and Zanzibar will delight the visitor. Peoples of many backgrounds live and work together.

49

A fishing boat with lateen-rigged sail proceeds downwind. The traditional Arab dhow, so common to the East African coast, has been the model for most sailing vessels for centuries. Often fishing boats are simply dugouts, with outrigger and lateen sails. These boats have no choice but to follow the wind and for this reason manoeuvrability is limited.

The attraction for the African to go to the big city is strong, so housing is in short supply. Shipping and exporting businesses occupy the plastered, gleaming white buildings along the waterfront. Dhows still ply the routes from Arabia to East Africa, and they are sailed by Arab and Shirazi people. The dhows still dock in their special area near the ocean liners which carry fuel and Tanzania's exports.

Workers in the cities usually travel by bicycle and bus. Buses connect all the major cities and towns. A common sight is a bus loaded with people inside, and bicycles and farm produce on the top. During the rainy season it is customary for passengers to help push, should the bus become stuck in mud.

Vendors set up their carts and stalls near the bus terminal, and large open-air markets line the streets. Taxis and station wagons (shooting brakes) thrive on their business of serving areas off the main roads. The major cities are also served by jets of the East African Air Lines, and smaller craft leave daily from Dar for the larger national game parks.

THE PEOPLE OF THE NORTH

Near Mount Kilimanjaro live the Chagga and Masai tribes. The countryside is fertile and blessed with pleasant climate and rainfall. It is dominated by "the mountain."

THE CHAGGAS

These people are of Bantu origin, and live in one of the most densely populated areas of Tanzania, close to the mountain. There are now nearly 400,000 Chaggas, which is an increase of over 50 per cent since 1950. Regarded as one of the most progressive tribes in the country,

This Swahili man from Tanzania's coast is playing a double reed instrument similar in structure and tone to the oboe.

the Chaggas are handsome and business-minded, and their coffee-growing co-operative societies are very successful.

THE MASAI

Though a small tribe (about one fifth the size of the Chagga) the Masai people are well known throughout the world. Their fierceness was respected by explorers during the 19th century, and their land was rarely disturbed.

Their villages are temporary, and they move when the grazing area is depleted. The Masai roam over a sparsely populated plain west of Kilimanjaro and north into Kenya. Their way of life and their independence are firmly established. Of Nilo-Hamitic origin, the Masai are related to the people of northern Kenya and Uganda.

LANGUAGES

The government of Tanzania adopted Swahili as its official language in 1967. It is a growing language that was developed along the coast by the traders—African and Arabian. Bantu words represent about two thirds of the vocabulary, and Arabic words most of the remainder. Some English has been adapted into it in the 20th century. Scholars have traced Swahili words to the coastal peoples' contact with Persian, Hindi, and Turkish also. The grammar and sentence structure are Bantu.

The Ngorongoro Crater serves as home for this Masai mother and her child. A Masai village, known as a "boma," usually consists of mud and wattle structures arranged in a circle (in background). The Masai are famous for their beadwork, as this heavily adorned woman shows.

51

Life in rural Tanzania generally begins at sunrise. Here, in a small coastal village containing temporary housing, a man begins the day by fetching water with an aluminium can called a "debe" in Swahili. Bicycles are widely used throughout Tanzania.

means "motor car"). Arabic words are most evident in numbers, days of the week, and trading phrases (for example, "sita" means "six," "saba" means "seven," "Alhamisi" means "Thursday," "ghali" means "expensive," and "rahisi" means "cheap").

There are, however, over 350,000 people in northern Tanzania around Arusha and in the northwest, whose mother tongue is Nilotic. A few thousand others speak a form of "click" language (having special clicking sounds). For them Swahili is a distinct, second language.

English is also taught in the schools, and it has been the language of instruction in secondary schools for many years.

MODERN TANZANIA

Many of the customs described so far have developed slowly over many generations, at a time when communications were slow and

Originally the language was written in Arabic, but it is now written in the Latin alphabet, and the Arabic characters are used only for ceremonial documents. As a spoken language it spread with the trade routes inland from the east coast, and is presently used by about 30,000,000 people, stretching as far west as Burundi and Zaire.

Children are usually taught the tribal language until they go to school. If the tribal language is one other than Swahili, this will be taught in the first few years of school. Swahili is closely related to the tribal languages of most children, and they learn it quickly.

Swahili contains vowel sounds like those of Spanish and Italian. Words are accented on the next to last syllable. One can find German words adapted during the early part of the 20th century ("shule" means "school") and English words adapted since World War II ("motakaa"

Ebony figures carved by the Makonde tribe are considered by many to be the finest artistic work in all East Africa. The Makonde people live in the dry highlands near the Mozambique border. They kept apart from the trading and enslavement of the coastal peoples, and today have emerged as one of the largest tribes in Tanzania.

Darkness does not hide the charm of Dar es Salaam at night as the buildings are brightly lighted. The parking problem exists in Dar es Salaam just as it does in cities throughout the world.

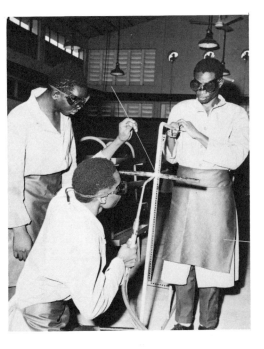

industrialization did not attract the attentions of tribal leaders. Today, changes are being made rapidly with foreign aid and exchange studies. Tribal leaders feel a sense of urgency in their quest for creating a modern nation with better food, clothing, and shelter for all the people.

As the many African tribesmen see the benefits of the new trade and communications, they too want a share of them—as most of the Europeans and Asians they see lead a comparatively affluent life. Citizens of all races have increased their efforts to create business and job opportunities for African tribesmen who are now filling the schools, eager to get on with "nation building."

Technical schools, such as this one in Dar es Salaam, help train young Tanzanians in tasks that were unknown to their fathers. Here welding techniques are being demonstrated.

Market day in the Arusha region is a busy occasion. Women dressed in bright outfits buy and sell bananas, coffee, tea, groundnuts (peanuts), fruits and vegetables. Sisal baskets are used as shopping bags to carry home the bargains of the day.

5. THE ECONOMY

AGRICULTURE

Like most African nations, Tanzania is mainly an agricultural country. From the land, Tanzanians provide their own food by growing rice, cassava, papayas, wheat, sweet potatoes, maize, sugar, tobacco and bananas on the small "shambas," or farms, that dot the countryside. None of these farm products are unusual enough to be exported. Very few changes have taken place in the farming methods used by the people of Tanzania over the last centuries. Tractors, threshers and other mechanized farm machines are much too expensive and, moreover, impractical because of the small sizes of plots. The government of Tanzania has encouraged the development of co-operative farms to increase agricultural output through mechanization.

MINERAL WEALTH

Poor roads and communication have been working against the development of the country's mineral wealth to its full potential. The largest deposits and most developed mining sites contain Tanzania's gem and industrial diamonds. Accounting for 77 per cent of the mineral income, diamonds are mined in the Shinyanga region of western Tanzania, near Lake Victoria, and the port of Mwanza. Some of the diamonds are of gem quality, the largest stone weighing slightly over 240 carats.

Other minerals found are gold (mostly in the

Moshi, a town at the foot of Mt. Kilimanjaro, is the hub of Tanzania's rich coffee industry. These Chagga ladies are carefully picking the berries which contain the beans.

southern highlands), salt, tin and mica. Gold is particularly important, accounting for 12 per cent of mineral income in Tanzania. In the future, Tanzania hopes to be linked to the rich copper mines of Zambia, which borders it on the southwest. Mainland China began construction of the "TanZam" railway line to link the two countries in 1970, and the work is scheduled to be completed in 1975. The railway line, covering 1,116 miles from Zambia to Dar es Salaam, will permit Zambia to ship its copper through Tanzania rather than through Rhodesia, Mozambique and Angola, all of which are governed by white minorities. This railroad could prove a boon to Tanzania, both in terms of its shipping industry and expanded

After the coffee beans have been extracted from the berries, they are dried by the strong tropical sun. These women are spreading the beans for faster drying.

55

This aerial view shows the Mwadui diamond mines in the Lake Victoria region. Diamonds are Tanzania's chief mineral export.

refining and manufacture. In addition to the railroad, the World Bank and the United States are financing and building a truck road parallel to the railroad.

EXPORTS

Tanzania's leading export product is sisal, a plant from whose fibres rope is made. Sisal mats and figurines are woven from the rope fibres taken from the plant. Sisal is not a native plant, a German scientist having introduced it in 1892 in the belief that the climate would be suitable for its growth. Out of 1,000 plants shipped to Tanzania from Florida, only 87 survived the trip across the ocean. It is from these 87 surviving plants that Tanzania can today claim to be the world's leading grower and producer of sisal. The exporting of sisal brings in much money, which in turn is used to purchase products that Tanzania does not have, such as automobiles, electrical products and machinery. Tanzania owes a lot to this unique plant that lives for about 10 years and weighs 300 pounds when fully grown!

Other Tanzanian exports include coffee, cotton, tea, groundnuts (peanuts) and pyrethrum. The rich coffee of Tanzania is quite

Tanzania's prime export, sisal, is here drying in the sunlight in the Morogoro region. The heart of the sisal industry is northeast of Morogoro at Tanga. After the fibres of sisal are dyed, they are often woven into rugs and mats.

popular in Europe and the money brought in is second only to sisal. The world coffee prices do fluctuate from year to year, and at times low prices have hurt Tanzania's economy. Cotton, the third most important export, is grown along the coast and on the plateau up to 4,000 feet above sea level. The cotton industry could be even more profitable for Tanzania if the processing and manufacturing could be carried on within the country rather than overseas. Now, clothing made of Tanzanian cotton is generally imported.

*ea picking is a painstaking
sk in the southern
ghlands. Tea is very
popular in East Africa and
cup of "chai" is always
fered to a visitor.*

Tea and groundnuts are grown extensively throughout the nation, but as cash crops are less important exports. The tea and groundnuts are consumed generally within the country. Pyrethrum, a type of chrysanthemum with finely divided and aromatic leaves, is a plant that offers great hope for the future. With all the interest shown around the world in getting safe pesticides and insecticides, pyrethrum has emerged as the raw material with the safest properties for man. Other insecticides such as DDT get rid of pests very well, but are harmful to the rest of the environment. Pyrethrum has proven to be harmful only to insects. This could prove quite a boon to Tanzania's economy in the future.

FORESTS

Tanzania has some small areas of dense forest, but most of the country is open woodland. The forests are extremely valuable because they help control soil erosion from flooding. Over 13 per cent of Tanzania is covered by trees. Some of the forests are located in unhealthy areas where the tzetze fly still exists and causes sleeping sickness. Generally, however, the forests are situated in the highest altitudes and high rainfall regions in northern and northeastern Tanzania. Southwestern Tanzania also has important standing timber. Most of the coastal region is covered with mangrove forests. The principal timbers to be cut are mahogany,

This young woman of the Meru tribe of northern Tanzania displays the daisy-like flowers of pyrethrum. The leaves and flowers are used in the production of safe insecticides. Pyrethrum is best grown in highlands between 6,000 and 8,000 feet above sea level.

57

These coastal girls are happily at work shelling cashew nuts for their parents. When the girls ar finished, their father will put the cashews in a sack and carry them to market. Regular shoes are luxury to be worn on such formal occasions as a visit to a town, family gatherings, and nationa celebrations. It is not uncommon to see Africans carrying their shoes when the roads are muddy.

Cotton is a leading crop of the small farmer, who sells it to co-operatives. Here women carry cotton to a co-operative buying post on Ukerewe Island in the Lake Region.

Old huts are bulldozed in Dar es Salaam to make way for new housing.

Acres and acres of tobacco grow on this farm in the Tabora region of western Tanzania. Most of the tobacco grown is consumed in East Africa, but a small portion is exported.

This busy cattle market is located in Songea, near the Mozambique border. In Tanzania, as well as i[n] other parts of East Africa, cattle are wealth. The more cattle a man owns the greater economic securit[y] he has through life. When daughters are married, the father receives a "bride price" of a negotiate[d] number of cattle. This dowry is set aside and used when the man's sons marry, school fees are needed, o[r] medical costs arise.

cedar, blackwood and camphorwood. The forests have been under government management since 1920 and improvements have been made in their use and conservation.

LIVESTOCK

Where the climate is poor and rainfall scarce, Tanzanians turn to cattle raising. Cattle are also important in the farming areas of Tanzania where they are used as investments and signs of prestige. The more cattle an African owns, the richer and more respected he is. The most prominent breed of cattle is the small, short-horned and humped variety called the zebu. Near Lake Victoria a long-horned breed of cattle called ankole is raised. In addition to cattle, Tanzanians are extensively involved i[n] raising sheep, goats and donkeys. Chickens ar[e] common all over Tanzania—the people usuall[y]

Zanzibar's second most important industry is the copra industry. The Zanzibaris above are supervising the drying of the coconut meat. Before they can be dried, the coconuts are cut in half and drained of the milk inside.

60

Masai cattle drink water from a man-made pond in northern Tanzania. The Masai people live mainly on the milk of the cow mixed with blood extracted from the veins of the living cows. The Masai keep this mixture in long gourds which they often take with them on grazing and hunting trips.

eat chicken to celebrate holidays or other special occasions such as visits.

ZANZIBAR'S ECONOMY

Zanzibar, like mainland Tanganyika, has an overwhelmingly agricultural economy. The islands of Zanzibar and Pemba have earned the nickname "The Islands of Cloves" as they produce most of the world's supply of cloves and clove oil. This spice comes from the dried flower bud of a tropical tree, and is widely used in the preparation of food around the world. Cloves account for 80 per cent of Zanzibar's exports, and naturally most of the people are involved in the industry either directly or indirectly. When one reaches the islands of

This busy cashew nut factory employs many women in Tanzania's southernmost port, Mtwara, near the Mozambique border. Here the cashews are sorted and inspections are made to ensure quality before the nuts are crated and shipped north.

Life has changed little ove[r] the centuries in the sleepy seaside villages of Zanziba[r].

Zanzibar and Pemba there is an unmistakable aroma of cloves in the air. The clove industry in Zanzibar dates back to the 1830's, when the island served as a base for Arab activity in East Africa. Sultan Seyyid Said introduced the spice to the island and, by the end of the 19th century, clove plantations on Zanzibar were producing about three-fourths of the world's supply.

Other important exports of Zanzibar include coconuts and copra. Copra, the dried meat of the coconut, is the source of coconut oil, which is often used in the making of soap. Zanzibar is also famous for its shells, pottery, jewelry, rope and mats. The island is a busy place and serves as an interesting tourist and historical attraction. Ancient palaces and beautiful gardens capture the curiosity of many visitors to the island.

The government of Zanzibar has pursued [a] policy of agricultural diversification by en[-]couraging the growing of rice for local con[-]sumption. The island depends too heavily o[n] the clove industry. Since independence, ri[ce] production has increased and the island [is] working towards self-sufficiency in this area.

One of the great thrills for mountaineers is to climb Mt. Kilimanjaro. The mountain consists of three peaks. Kibo (shown here), the highest and most photographed, is an almost perfect cone. Mawenzi is a jagged, ancient volcanic peak to the east. Shira, at 13,140 ft., is the smallest and has numerous small craters. It usually takes five days to climb Kibo, and the best months are January and July, after the rains. Difficult rock conditions and snow limit this challenging ascent to experienced climbers only.

Elephants make their way across the scrub land of Lake Manyara National Park as a storm threatens. Visitors at the modern hotel can view them from the top of the escarpment through magnifying glasses. Cars may be driven throughout the park, but motorists are urged to yield the right of way to herds such as this.

TOURISM IN TANZANIA

Tanzania's economic planners foresee a great future for tourism, and already many people are employed in tourist-related activities in hotels, transportation, restaurants, souvenir shops and game parks. To lure tourists, the government has passed strict laws against poaching to conserve wildlife and protect the land. Many tourists from Britain, West Germany, the U.S. and Asia have already come to Tanzania and new tourists are being induced to come by lower air fares and packaged plans.

Lake Tanganyika, second deepest in the world, has over 200 varieties of fish, including perch, and tiger fish.

63

Boys do a ceremonial sna[ke]
dance.

Hunters once travelled to
Tanzania to kill wild life.
Since game is now
protected, hunters come with
cameras, not guns, and ride
in safari coaches like this
one.